D1094048

THE POETRY OF PREACHING

THE POETRY OF PREACHING

Compiled by
Dr. Clyde H. Box

P. O. Box 1099, Murfreesboro, TN 37133

Earnest effort has been made to locate authors and owners and to secure permission from them for the use of their material. Any errors or omissions that may have been made are unintentional and will be corrected in future printings if notification is sent to the publisher, Sword of the Lord.

▶

Printed and Bound in the United States of America

CONTENTS

DEDICATION

To my precious wife, Betty, without whom life
would not be worth living

But for love I'd never know
  The happiness of sharing.
But for love I'd never know
  The tenderness of caring.
But for love I'd never know
  The joy of dreams come true.
But for love I'd never know
  The miracle of you.

—Clyde H. Box

Bible

IT MUST BE FROM GOD

The Holy Bible must have been
Inspired of God and not of men.
I could not if I would, believe
That good men wrote it to deceive;
And bad men could not if they would,
And surely would not if they could,
Proceed to write a book so good.
And certainly no crazy man
Could e'er conceive its wondrous plan.
And pray, what other kinds of men
Than do these three groups comprehend?
Hence it must be that God inspired
The Word which souls of prophets fired.

—Author unknown

THE BIBLE

Do you treat the Word of God
　　As you treat no other book—
Just a verse or two today,
　　Just a short, impatient look?

Try a different approach;
　　Feast on manna from above;
Kneel and read the Bible through,
　　And you'll find eternal Love.

—Clyde H. Box

1

FRONTISPIECE

Down in the wood-clad hills,
    All somber and stately and old,
Men go to burrow in the ground,
    To seek for gems of gold.

I burrowed in a richer bed;
    I struck a richer ore
Of gems of gold that never fail,
    That last forevermore.

I mined deep down within God's Word
    Where riches all abound;
God helped me, and my heart rejoiced;
    His gems of gold I found.

And now I want to share with you
    The wonders of my find.
Come! Help yourself! This gold is yours,
    All ready, all refined.

—Selected

THE BIBLE'S PEDIGREE

The Bible is, we plainly see;
Then it must have a pedigree.
It either is a Book divine,
Or men to make it did combine.
Suppose the latter; then they must ₋
Either be wicked men or just:
Take either case, and you will see
A proof of its divinity.

If wicked men composed this Book,
Surely their senses they forsook;
For they the righteous man defend
And curse the bad from end to end.
If righteous, then they change their name,
For they the authorship disclaim
And often say, "Thus saith the LORD,"
And testify, "It is His Word."
If it be not, they tell a lie
And all their righteousness deny.

—Author unknown

THE PRECIOUS BIBLE

Though the cover is worn
And the pages are torn,
And though places bear traces of tears;
Yet more precious than gold
Is the Book, worn and old,
That can shatter and scatter my fears.

When I prayerfully look
In the precious old Book,
Many pleasures and treasures I see;
Many tokens of love
From the Father above,
Who is nearest and dearest to me.

The old Book is my Guide,
'Tis a Friend by my side;
It will lighten and brighten my way;
And each promise I find
Soothes and gladdens my mind
As I read it and heed it each day.

—Anonymous

THE ANVIL OF GOD'S WORD

Last eve I paused beside the blacksmith's door,
　And heard the anvil ring the vesper chime;
Then looking in, I saw upon the floor
　Old hammers worn with beating years of time.

"How many anvils have you had," said I,
　"To wear and batter all these hammers so?"
"Just one," said he; and then with twinkling eye,
　"The anvil wears the hammers out, you know."

"And so," I thought, "the anvil of God's Word
　For ages skeptic blows have beat upon;
Yet though the noise of falling blows was heard,
　The Anvil is unharmed, the hammers gone."

　　　　　　　　　　—John Clifford, D.D.

Character

WOUNDED BUT NOT SLAIN

I'm wounded now, but I'm not slain;
  I'm bruised and faint, they say;
Just let me lie and bleed a while;
  I'll not be long this way.

My spirit's low, and my eyes flow;
  My heart is sad and sore;
But when my pen'ent tears are gone,
  I'll stand and fight some more.

I'll bind these wounds, I'll dry these tears,
  I'll close this bleeding vein;
I'll not lie here and weep and die;
  I'll rise and fight again.

'Twas yesterday I bowed so low,
  Was weak from tears and pain;
Today I'm strong, my fears are gone;
  Today I fight again.

—Author unknown

KEEP GOING

We have not wings and cannot fly;
We were not made to soar the sky.
So we must walk to meet our goals,
To reach the lost and hungry souls.

The goals great men have reached and kept
   Were not attained by sudden flight.
But they, while other workers slept,
   Kept going on throughout the night.

—Clyde H. Box

TODAY

With every rising of the sun,
Think of your life as just begun.
The past has cancelled and buried deep
All yesterdays. There let them sleep.
Concern yourself with but today.
Grasp it, and teach it to obey
Your will and plan. Since time began
Today has been the friend of man.
You and Today! A soul sublime
And the great heritage of time.
With God Himself to bind the twain,
Go forth, brave heart! Attain! attain!

—Anonymous

LITTLE BY LITTLE

Little by little all things grow—
Plants and trees—from the seed we sow:
The beginning of life is under the ground,
In darkness and silence all profound;
Then a tiny shoot comes up to the light,
And the plant increases in beauty and might.

Little by little bad habits grow—
How they begin, we scarcely know.
A little wrong act, a little false word,
One pleasant drink in the poison-cup stirred,
Repeated once in awhile again,
And soon we are caught in a cruel chain.

Little by little good principles grow,
Steady and sure though sometimes slow:
A little act done because it is right
Soon comes to be choice—a real delight—
Until second nature it grows to be,
And we walk in its light and liberty.

—Author unknown

THE FEW

The easy roads are crowded
  And the level roads are jammed;
The pleasant little rivers
  With the drifting folk are crammed.

But out yonder where it's rocky,
  Where you get a better view,
You will find the ranks are thinning
  And the travelers are few.

Where the going's smooth and pleasant
  You will always find the throng,
For the many, more's the pity,
  Seem to like to drift along.

But the steeps that call for courage
  And the task that's hard to do,
In the end result in glory
  For the never-wavering few.

—Edgar A. Guest

Christic, God

THE GOD-MAN

Someone says, "How can this be? He was the 'God-Man'!"
If He was not a man—who was that Babe in Bethlehem's
manger?
If He was not God—why did a choir of angels come down
from Heaven and sing at His birth?
If He was not a man—who called Himself "the Son of man"?
If He was not God—who said, "I and my Father are one"?
If He was not a man—who washed the disciples' feet?
If He was not God—who washed them from their sins in
His own blood?
If He was not a man—who was it that wept at Lazarus' tomb?
If He was not God—who called Lazarus forth from that tomb?
If He was not a man—who hungered on the mountainside?
If He was not God—who fed a hungry multitude on that
same mountainside with a little boy's lunch?
If He was not a man—who stood before Pilate when Pilate
said, "Behold the man"?
If He was not God—who caused Pilate to wash his hands
and say, "I find no fault in this man"?
If He was not a man—whose hands and feet were nailed to
the cross?
If He was not God—who rent the veil in the temple?
If He was not a man—who hung on the cross?
If He was not God—who moved the earth from its founda-
tions?
If He was not a man—who cried out from the cross, "I
thirst"?
If He was not God—who gave the woman at the well living
water?
If He was not a man—who cried out, "My God, my God,

why hast thou forsaken me?"
If He was not God—who said, "Father, forgive them; for
they know not what they do"?
If He was not a man—who was buried in Joseph's tomb?
If He was not God—who came forth from that same tomb
three days later?
I say to you today, HE WAS MAN! HE WAS GOD! HE WAS
THE GOD-MAN,
And He is mine!

—Clyde H. Box

AT THE CROSS

Alas! and did my Saviour bleed?
    And did my Sov'reign die?
Would He devote that sacred head
    For such a worm as I?

Was it for crimes that I had done
    He groaned upon the tree?
Amazing pity! Grace unknown!
    And love beyond degree!

Well might the sun in darkness hide
    And shut his glories in;
When Christ, the mighty Maker, died
    For man, the creature's, sin.

Thus might I hide my blushing face
    While His dear cross appears,
Dissolve my heart in thankfulness
    And melt my eyes to tears.

But drops of grief can ne'er repay
    The debt of love I owe;
Here, Lord, I give myself away,
    'Tis all that I can do.

—Charles Wesley

SIMON PETER'S SOLILOQUY

'Why are you cast down, O my soul?'
Why indeed! Because of HIM! That's why!
I'd rather DIE than live through misery like that again!
'Put up your sword,' He said, as to a child—
Rebuked for being BRAVE!
What kind of Man condemns the courage
He Himself inspired?
There they go—
That treacherous horde...
Their angry torches seem like tiny sparks from here.
And now they fade...as does my hope!
"No! I'm NOT! I am NOT His!"
Why should I be, when He disclaimed His
own disciple by that act?
He HEALED that wretched ear!
Why did He sport His miracles for THEM?
With but a word He could have sliced the neck I missed—
INSTEAD...Good—a fire,
I hope I won't be recognized again...
My hands are numb...This night is bitter...black.
So is my soul.
"No!" I said. "I DON'T KNOW HIM!"
I thought I did—no more! Not now!
For when He meekly left with them,
His footsteps stamped my soul into the ground!
He once defied the moneychangers,
stilled wild storms and men.
NOW LOOK—He's weak. And bound.
I repeat—"I DON'T KNOW WHO HE IS!"
He turns this way...He sees me...
He HEARD me!
WHAT! A rooster crows...A rooster crows!

—Selected

DEATH MEETS THE MASTER

Father Time met pale King Death
   Sittin' by a tomb.
"Hello, old friend, I guess you're here
   To seal somebody's doom."

"You might say that," sly Death replied;
   A smile slid up his face.
"Inside repose that Jesus Man
   Who said He'd save the race.

"And you, Time, why you stoppin' here?
   Don't you have things to do?"
"I come each day to draw the veil
   And let the mornin' through.

"Say, why you watchin' jus' one grave,
   With all your vast domain?
Looks like you'd be out ramblin' 'round
   An' smitin' folks with pain."

"Well, this one's something special:
   He challenged me, they say.
Said He'd rest here just three days,
   Then stir and walk away.

"Now I'm the conqueror, you know;
   They don't talk up to me.
When I steps in to cut 'em down,
   It's for eternity."

"I can testify to that,"
   Responded Father Time.
"I ain't seen one shake off the dust
   Since you been in your prime.

"Well, I got other things to do;
  I must be on my way.
I'll see you when I come back by
  To make another day."

So whiskered Time went up the hill
  To bid the sun to rise,
And left Death standin' by the tomb
  Lookin' strong an' wise.

Next day Time ambled by again.
  "An' how are things?" he queried.
"Kinda quiet," Death replied.
  "I'm startin' to be wearied.

"I won't be here when you come by
  About this time tomorrow.
I'm anxious to be on my way
  An' spread some grief and sorrow."

So Father Time was quite surprised
  When he came back to see
Death a-quiverin' on the ground
  In frightful agony!

His eyes were set, his throat was marked,
  His clothes in disarray.
It wasn't difficult to see
  That Death had had his day.

"What happened, Death?" asked Father Time.
  "What makes you look so bad?
I've never seen you shake this way
  Or seem so scared and sad."

Death pulled himself up on a rock,

A-lookin' sick an' humble,
Hung his head an' wrung his hands;
 And Time could hear him mumble:

"Was sittin' here before the dawn,
 About to take my stroll.
When all at once this whole wide world
 Began to reel and roll.

"That rollin' stone jumped off the door;
 An' skipped on down the hill.
Then everything grew dark and quiet;
 Seemed like the earth stood still.

"I saw Him standin' in the door;
 He didn't move or speak.
Just looked at me, an' all at once
 I felt so tired and weak.

"He came and got a hold on me
 An' threw me to the groun',
Put His foot here on my neck,
 Then took my keys an' crown.

"Two angels came to talk with Him;
 They glistened like the sun.
He said, 'The plan's all finished now;
 Redemption's work is done.'

"And as they passed the garden gate
 I heard Him say just then,
He's settin' free the captives,
 And givin' gifts to men."

Time and Death met once again
 Off yonder by the gate.

"It's good to see you," said old Time.
  "I've wondered 'bout your fate."

"I'm just a lowly servant now;
  There's little time to roam;
I just push open this old gate
  And help the saints get Home!"

—Elwood McQuaid
  The Friends of Israel Gospel
  Ministry, Inc.
  Bellmawr, N.J.
  Used by permission

TO DESTROY HIS NAME

(From the Sermon "The Fragrance of Christ")

Destroy that glorious Name of Christ—
Of Him who was so sacrificed
For man because he could not pay
The price to take his sin away?
The birds would sing it sweetly then
Until it's written once again
On every heart of men on earth
Because of its eternal worth.

Destroy that Name that God has given?
You'd have to remove the gates of Heaven,
The streets, the buildings, every stone;
For on them is that Name alone;
But still in Heaven that Name would be,
For Jesus is its Light, you see.

Destroy that Name that's over all?
Before that Name each man must fall.
Tear out each verse of every page
Of the greatest book of every age,
In every language found on earth,
Of every tongue of every birth;
But then some stone in some strange land
Would rise and shout, "The Son of Man!"

Destroy that Name? It cannot be
Until each star in heaven flee,
Until each planet is erased
That was by Him so rightly placed;
And even then the universe

Would speak of Him who cured the curse.

For by His Name so sweet, so pure,
Our life on earth we can endure
Until one day in Heaven we find
His Name still stands—it's yours—it's mine.

—Clyde H. Box

THE LORD IN THE BIBLE

I see my Lord in the Bible whenever I chance to look.
He is the theme of the Bible, the center and heart of the
  Book.

He is the Rose of Sharon; He is the Lily fair.
Whenever I open the Bible, the Lord of the Bible is there.

He in the Book's beginning gave to the earth its form.
He is the ark of safety that bears the brunt of the storm;

The burning bush of the desert, the budding of Aaron's
  rod—
Whenever I open the Bible, I see the Son of God.

The ram upon Mount Moriah, the ladder from earth to sky,
The scarlet cord in the window, the serpent lifted high;

The smitten rock of the desert, the Shepherd with staff and
  crook—
Whenever I open the Bible, I see my Lord in the Book.

He is the seed of the woman, the Saviour virgin born;
He is the Son of David whom men rejected with scorn;

The Lord of eternal glory whom John the apostle saw,
The light of Celestial City, the Lamb without spot or flaw;

The Bridegroom coming at midnight for whom His people
  look—
Whenever I open the Bible, I see my Lord in the Book.

—Author unknown

THAT NIGHT

That night when in the Judean skies
   The mystic star dispensed its light,
A blind man moved in his sleep—
   And dreamed that he had sight.

That night when shepherds heard the song
   Of hosts angelic choiring near,
A deaf man stirred in slumber's spell—
   And dreamed that he could hear!

That night when in the cattle stall
   Slept Child and mother cheek by jowl,
A cripple turned his twisted limbs—
   And dreamed that he was whole.

That night when o'er the newborn Babe
   The tender Mary rose to lean,
A loathsome leper smiled in sleep—
   And dreamed that he was clean.

That night when to the mother's breast
   The little King was held secure,
A harlot slept a happy sleep—
   And dreamed that she was pure!

That night when in the manger lay
   The Sanctified who came to save,
A man moved in the sleep of death—
   And dreamed there was no grave.

          —Author unknown

"COME FORTH!"

Before the tomb Christ stood one day
And dried the people's tears away
As He spoke forth in mighty voice
That made Judea's hills rejoice,
          "Come forth!"

Inside the tomb Christ lay one morn;
Defeated seemed salvation's horn;
But God the Father spoke the word,
And this He said tho' no man heard,
          "Come forth!"

Inside the tomb of sin I lay,
The price of sin I had to pay;
But Christ, the raiser of the dead,
Spoke to my poor bound soul and said,
          "Come forth!"

And when that great and final sound
Shall raise our loved ones from the ground,
'Twill be the last time we shall hear
That glorious sound upon our ear:
          "Come forth!"

                              —Author unknown

HOW DO I KNOW?

How do I know that Christ is risen?
   What proof have I to give?
He touched my life one blessed day,
   And I began to live.

How do I know He left the tomb
   That Easter long ago?
I met Him just this morning, and
   My life is all aglow.

How do I know that endless life
   He gained that day for me?
His life within is proof enough
   Of immortality.

How do I know that Christ still lives
   Rich blessings to impart?
I know it's true because He lives
   And reigns within my heart.

                    —Eugene M. Harrison

WHAT I THINK OF JESUS

If asked what of Jesus I think,
   Tho' still my best thoughts are but poor,
I say He's my Meat and my Drink,
   My Life, my Strength and my Store;
My Shepherd, my Trust and my Friend,
   My Saviour from sin and from thrall,
My Hope from beginning to end,
   My Portion, my Lord and my All.

                    —John Newton

THE CROSS WAS HIS OWN

They borrowed a bed to lay His head
    When Christ the Lord came down;
They borrowed the ass in the mountain pass
    For Him to ride to town;
But the crown that He wore and the cross that He bore
    Were His own—the cross was His own.

He borrowed the bread when the crowd He fed
    On the grassy mountainside;
He borrowed the dish of broken fish
    With which He satisfied;
But the crown that He wore and the cross that He bore
    Were His own—the cross was His own.

He borrowed the ship in which to sit
    To teach the multitude;
He borrowed a nest in which to rest—
    He had never a home so rude;
But the crown that He wore and the cross that He bore
    Were His own—the cross was His own.

He borrowed a room on His way to the tomb,
    The Passover lamb to eat;
They borrowed a cave for Him a grave;
    They borrowed a winding sheet;
But the crown that He wore and the cross that He bore
    Were His own—they rightly were mine.

               —L. M. Hollinsworth

HE TOOK THE VINEGAR FOR ME

He's bruised and battered; strength is gone,
　　Suspended in disgrace.
Between creation, heaven and earth,
　　He hangs. He takes my place.

From fevered body racked with pain,
　　His cry is heard, "I thirst."
The rain from heav'n? The ocean deep?
　　Which will He beckon first?

He beckons none...though need is great;
　　Yet foe has heard His plea.
With bitter sponge they press His lips.
　　He takes the drink for me.

The vinegar of poverty;
　　The bitterness of pain;
The drink of friend betraying Him;
　　The vinegar of shame.

O Christ, my Source of living water,
　　By which I'll never thirst again,
Today He took the drink for me,
　　The vinegar of sin.

　　　　　　　　—Patti Appleby
　　　　　　　　May 5, 1982

Consecration and Surrender

FOLLOW ME

Follow Me, and I will make you...
    Make you speak My words with power;
Make you channels of My mercy;
    Make you helpful every hour.

Follow Me, and I will make you...
    Make you what you cannot be;
Make you loving, trustful, godly;
    Make you even like to Me.

—L.S.P.

FOR JESUS' SAKE

When often, like a wayward child,
    I murmur at His will,
Then this sweet word, "For Jesus' sake,"
    My restless heart can still.

I bow my head, and gently led,
    His easy yoke I take;
And all the day and all the way,
An echo in my heart shall say,
    "For Jesus' sake."

—Selected

I HEARD THE VOICE OF JESUS SAY

I heard the voice of Jesus say,
  "Come unto Me and rest;
Lay down, thou weary one, lay down
  Thy head upon My breast."

I came to Jesus as I was,
  Weary and worn and sad;
I found in Him a resting-place,
  And He has made me glad.

I heard the voice of Jesus say,
  "Behold, I freely give
The living water—thirsty one,
  Stoop down and drink, and live."

I came to Jesus, and I drank
  Of that life-giving stream;
My thirst was quenched, my soul revived,
  And now I live in Him.

I heard the voice of Jesus say,
  "I am this dark world's Light;
Look unto Me—thy morn shall rise,
  And all thy day be bright."

I looked to Jesus, and I found
  In Him my Star, my Sun;
And in that Light of life I'll walk,
  Till trav'ling days are done.

—Horatius Bonar

IT DIDN'T JUST HAPPEN

Things don't just happen to children of God;
   They're part of a wonderful plan.
The troubles, reverses, the sorrows, the rod
   Are strokes of the Great Sculptor's hand.
When some dread accident strikes you a blow
   And you worry and fret and demand,
Why try so hard the mystery to know?
   It's not just an accident; it's planned.

Have you been dropped from a place of power?
   Do you wonder and reprimand?
Don't rebel, but look to Him in that hour;
   This didn't just happen; it's planned.
Persecution, tribulation come down like a storm;
   Friends disappoint and withstand;
At last all alone, bewildered, forlorn,
   You look, and He says, "This is planned."

                 —Author unknown

JUST TO BE TENDER

Just to be tender, just to be true,
Just to be glad the whole day through,
Just to be merciful, just to be mild,
Just to be trustful as a child;
Just to be gentle, kind and sweet,
Just to be helpful with willing feet,
Just to be cheery when things go wrong,
Just to drive sadness away with song;
Whether the hour is dark or bright,
Just to be loyal to God and right,
Just to believe that God knows best,
Just in His promises ever to rest;
Just to let love be our daily key—
That is God's will for you and me.

—Author unknown

CHIEF OF SINNERS

Chief of sinners though I be,
Christ is all in all to me;
Lived that I might never die,
Died that I might reign on high.
As the branch is to the vine,
I am His and He is mine.

—Author unknown

COULD I BE CALLED A CHRISTIAN?

Could I be called a Christian if everybody knew
My secret thoughts and failings and everything I do?
Oh, could they see the likeness of Christ in me each day,
Or could they hear Him speaking in every word I say?

Could I be called a Christian if other folk could know
That I am found in places where Jesus would not go?
Oh, could they hear His echo in every song I sing?
In eating, drinking, dressing—is Christ in everything?

Could I be called a Christian if judged by what I read,
By all my recreations and every thought and deed?
Could I be counted Christlike as I now work and play—
Unselfish, kind, forgiving to others every day?

—Selected

MY HANDS

My hands were filled with many things
    That I did precious hold,
As any treasure of a king's—
    Silver or gems or gold.
The Master came and touched my hands,
    The scars were in His own.
And at His feet my treasures sweet
    Fell shattered, one by one.
"I must have empty hands," said He,
"Wherewith to work My works through thee."

My hands were growing feverish
    And cumbered with much care!
Trembling with haste and eagerness,
    Nor folded oft in prayer.
The Master came and touched my hands,
    With healing in His own;
And calm and still to do His will
    They grew—the fever gone.
"I must have quiet hands," said He,
"Wherewith to work My works through thee."

My hands were stained with marks of toil,
    Defiled with dust of earth;
And I my work did ofttimes soil
    And render little worth.
The Master came and touched my hands,
    And crimson were His own.
But when, amazed, on mine I gazed,
    Lo, every stain was gone!
"I must have cleansed hands," said He,
"Wherewith to work My works through thee."

—Author unknown

I MET THE MASTER

I had walked life's way with an easy tread,
Had followed where comforts and pleasures led,
Until one day in a quiet place
I met the Master face to face.

With station and rank and wealth for my goal,
Much thought for my body but none for my soul,
I had entered to win in life's mad race,
When I met the Master face to face.

I had built my castles and reared them high,
Till their towers pierced the blue of the sky;
I had vowed to rule with an iron mace,
When I met the Master face to face.

I met Him and knew Him and blushed to see
That His eyes full of sorrow were fixed on me;
And I faltered and fell at His feet that day,
While my castles melted and vanished away.

Melted and vanished, and in their place
Naught else did I see but the Master's face;
And I cried aloud, "Oh, make me meet
To follow the steps of Thy wounded feet!"

My thought is now for the souls of men;
I have lost my life to find it again,
E'er since one day in a quiet place
I met the Master face to face.

—Author unknown

OBEDIENCE

I said, "Let me walk in the fields."
  He said, "Nay, walk in the town."
I said, "There are no flowers there."
  He said, "No flowers, but a crown."

I said, "But the sky is black;
  There is nothing but noise and din."
But He wept as He sent me back;
  "There is more," He said; "there is sin."

I said, "But the air is thick,
  And fogs are veiling the sun."
He answered, "Yet hearts are sick,
  And souls in the dark undone."

I said, "I shall miss the light,
  And friends will miss me, they say."
He answered me, "Choose tonight
  If I am to miss you, or they."

I pleaded for time to be given;
  He said, "Is it hard to decide?
It will not seem hard in Heaven
  To have followed the steps of your Guide."

I cast one look at the fields,
  Then set my face to the town;
He said, "My child, do you yield?
  Will you leave the flowers for the crown?"

Then into His hand went mine,
  And into my heart came He;
And I walk in the light divine
  The path I had feared to see!

—George MacDonald

Consolation and Comfort

HE GIVETH MORE GRACE

He giveth more grace when the burdens grow greater;
   He sendeth more strength when the labors increase.
To added affliction He addeth His mercy;
   To multiplied trials, His multiplied peace.

When we have exhausted our store of endurance,
   When our strength has failed ere the day is half done,
When we reach the end of our hoarded resources,
   Our Father's full giving is only begun.

His love has no limit; His grace has no measure;
   His power no boundary known unto men;
For out of His infinite riches in Jesus
   He giveth and giveth and giveth again.

—Annie Johnson Flint

HEALING TOUCH

The touch that heals the broken heart
   Is never felt above;
His angels know His blessedness;
   His wayworn saints, His love.

LEAN HARD

"Cast thy burden upon the Lord, *and he
shall sustain thee."*—Ps. 55:22.

Child of My love, lean hard,
And let Me feel the pressure of thy care;
I know thy burden, child; I shaped it,
Poised it in Mine own hand, made no proportion
In its weight to thine unaided strength;
For even as I laid it on, I said,
"I shall be near, and while she leans on Me,
This burden shall be Mine, not hers;
So shall I keep My child within the circling arms
Of My own love." Here lay it down, nor fear
To impose it on a shoulder which upholds
The government of worlds. Yet closer come;
Thou art not near enough. I would embrace thy care,
So I might feel My child reposing on My breast;
Thou lovest Me? I knew it. Doubt not then;
But loving Me, lean hard.

—Paul Pastnor

JESUS KNOWS

He knows the thorny way,
    The bodily distress;
He knows these tents decay,
    And He stays by to bless.
We're cheered along meanwhile
By His unclouded smile—
        Jesus knows!

He knows the pains and aches,
    The sight that's growing dim;
Account of all He takes,
    For we belong to Him.
The trembling knees He'll hold,
His arms do us enfold—
        Jesus knows!

He knows the hidden grief,
    The solitude He feels;
He gives us sweet relief,
    Joy afterward it yields.
Blessing for us ensured
By Him who much endured—
        Jesus knows!

—Author unknown

THE TOUCH OF HIS WONDERFUL HANDS

How blest to know He who created
　　Each rose and each new budding tree,
In loving compassion has said,
　　"My grace is sufficient for thee."

Whatever the heartache or sorrow,
　　How good to know God understands
And that there's new hope for tomorrow
　　In the touch of His wonderful hands!

　　　　　　　　　　—Author unknown

RELIEF FROM MY BURDEN

I prayed for relief from my burden,
　　Asked the Lord to take it away,
But I grew unsettled and doubtful,
　　For my burden grew harder each day.

Then I changed the note of my praying
　　And asked for the Master alone;
Then turned to take up my burden,
　　And lo, my burden was gone!

　　　　　　　　　　—Anonymous

HE MAKETH NO MISTAKE

My Father's way may twist and turn,
　My heart may throb and ache;
But in my soul I'm glad I know
　He maketh no mistake.

My cherished plans may go astray,
　My hopes may fade away;
But still I'll trust my Lord to lead,
　For He doth know the way.

Though night be dark, and it may seem
　That day will never break,
I'll pin my faith, my all in Him:
　He maketh no mistake.

There's so much now I cannot see,
　My eyesight's far too dim;
But come what may, I'll simply trust
　And leave it all to Him.

For by and by the mist will lift,
　And plain it all He'll make;
Through all the way, though dark to me,
　He made not one mistake.

　　　　　　　　　—A. M. Overton

Death and Heaven

IN AND OUT

Eden had a way out—
But no way in.

Heaven has a way in—
But no way out.

STEPPING ASHORE

Oh, think to step ashore,
  And find it Heaven;
To clasp a hand outstretched,
  And find it God's hand!
To breathe new air,
  And that, celestial air;
To feel refreshed,
  And find it immortality;
Ah, think to step from storm and stress
  To one unbroken calm:
To awake, and find it Home.

—Robert E. Selle

A SHINING LIGHT

In the books of Genesis and Revelation, preachers are referred to as STARS—STARS who are to light up this old dark world for Jesus Christ. Daniel 12:3 says, "And they that be wise shall shine as the brightness of the firmament; and they that turn many to righteousness as the STARS for ever and ever."

And every star has his place. The Sword of the Lord was Curtis Hutson's place to shine. And he got his light from the One who said, "I am the light of the world." He stayed so close to the Source that he reflected and radiated that Light.

The best way to scatter the darkness is to light a light. And by God's grace, under the leadership of Dr. Curtis Hutson, the Sword has lit up the world for Christ. As Job said, "He maketh a path to shine after him."

One time a captain in the English army fell wounded on the battlefield. As he lay dying, he said to his general, "I led them straight, sir."

God made Dr. Hutson a captain of truth against error. His life has been spent on the battlefield of this world fighting the good fight of faith.

One day his battle will be over, and he will lay down the "Sword," kneel at the feet of our Great Commander, look into His sweet face and say, "Lord Jesus, I led the people straight."

So many times we hear people glorify the medical profession or the legal profession or the political profession, but I glorify my own. I believe that being a God-called preacher of the Gospel is the greatest calling in the world.

I have seen preachers at the bedsides of dying saints. I have heard their words of comfort. I have heard them in their pulpits as they plead with people to come to Jesus. I have seen them kneel with sinners and lead them to Christ. I have seen them, heard them and watched their lives; and I want you to know that a grander group of men never breathed—men like John Rice...Lester Roloff...Lee Roberson...Bob Gray...and Curtis Hutson.

So God did not strain when He called them STARS—especially this one I lovingly call "my brother." He is not a comet that flashed for awhile, then went out...No, he shines and will shine for Jesus throughout the eternal ages.

He shined too bright for this world.

Written by Dr. Clyde H. Box
For Dr. Curtis Hutson

"THE CEDAR IS FALLEN"

Zechariah 11:2
In Zechariah, chapter 11 and verse 2, the Bible says:
"Howl, fir tree; for the cedar is fallen."

When a small tree falls in the forest, no one gets too excited about it. The birds keep on flying from tree to tree and singing as if nothing has happened. The deer does not lift its mouth from drinking in the creek.

But when a cedar, the glory of the forest that has been standing for centuries, falls because of decay, the whole forest knows. Every living thing in the forest hears its fall.

A short time ago an axman dressed in black went into the forest of men. In the past he has cut down many a tall tree of a man—Spurgeon...Moody...Finney...Bob Jones, Sr....Bill Rice...R. G. Lee.

But this time the axman aimed his blade at one we all knew and loved and honored and depended upon.

He struck again and again until the cedar—which had withstood the blasts of trouble and trial and abuse—dropped into the dust.

And the sound of his fall resounded around the world! "John R. Rice is dead!" "The cedar is fallen!"

And the text echoes in our hearts: 'Howl, fir tree; the mighty cedar is fallen.'

The saddest words the Israelites ever heard were: "Moses my servant is dead." And the saddest words Fundamentalism will ever hear are: "John R. Rice is dead."

Let neither pen nor tongue by useless criticism add one drop to our cup of grief—it is filled to the brim already.

"THE CEDAR IS FALLEN!" "JOHN R. RICE IS DEAD!"

Now we lay his body away to await the trumpet sound.

His right hand is closed because there are no more heroic words for it to write for THE SWORD OF THE LORD.

His lips are shut, for there are no more sermons for him to preach. His heart is quiet—it will never break again.

I put on his grave no wreath, but a scroll plain and white, half open so you may read it. It says: "He that goeth forth and weepeth, bearing precious seed, shall doubtless come again with rejoicing, bringing his sheaves with him."

And as we walk from his grave, a voice seems to come from Heaven saying:

"HOWL, FIR TREE...THE CEDAR IS FALLEN."

—Clyde H. Box
December 29, 1980

SHOULD YOU GO FIRST

Should you go first and I remain
    To walk the road alone,
I'll live in memory's garden, dear,
    With happy days we've known.
In spring I'll wait for roses red,
    When fades the lilac's blue;
In early fall when brown leaves call,
    I'll catch a glimpse of you.

Should you go first and I remain
    For battles to be fought,
Each thing you've touched along the way
    Will be a hallowed spot.
I'll hear your voice, I'll see your smile,
    Though blindly I may grope.
The memory of your helping hand
    Will buoy me on with hope.

Should you go first and I remain
    To finish with the scroll,
No length'ning shadows shall creep in
    To make this life seem droll.
We've known so much of happiness;
    We've had our cup of joy;
And memory is one gift of God
    That death cannot destroy.

Should you go first and I remain,
    One thing I'd have you do:
Walk slowly down the path of death,
    For soon I'll follow you.
I'll want to know each step you take

That I may walk the same,
For someday down that lonely road
You'll hear me call your name.

—Albert Kennedy Rowswell

How a Famous Hymn Was Written

As Tennyson's nurse was sitting one day at his bedside, sharing to a degree the general anxiety about the patient, she said to him suddenly:

"You have written a great many poems, sir, but I have never heard anybody say that there is a hymn among them all. I wish, sir, you would write a hymn while you are lying on your sickbed. It might help and comfort many a poor sufferer."

The next morning, when the nurse had taken her quiet place at the bedside, the poet handed her a scrap of paper, saying, "Here is the hymn you wished me to write."

She took it from his hands with expressions of gratified thanks. It proved to be "Crossing the Bar," the poem that was sung in Westminster Abbey at Tennyson's funeral and which has touched so many hearts.

CROSSING THE BAR

Sunset and evening star
   And one clear call for me!
And may there be no moaning of the bar
   When I put out to sea,

But such a tide as moving seems asleep,
   Too full for sound or foam,
When that which drew from out the boundless deep
   Turns again home.

Twilight and evening bell,
   And after that the dark!

And may there be no sadness of farewell
   When I embark.

For tho' from out our bourne of Time and Place
   The flood may bear me far,
I hope to see my Pilot face to face
   When I have crossed the bar.

—Alfred Tennyson

THE DEATH OF A CHILD

The golden gates were open,
  And heavenly angels smiled,
And with their tuneful harpstring
  Welcomed the little child.

They shouted high and holy,
  "A child hath entered in,
And safe from all temptation,
  A soul is sealed from sin."

They led him through the golden streets
  On to the King of Kings,
And a glory fell upon him
  From the rustling of their wings.

The Saviour smiled upon him
  As none on earth had smiled,
And Heav'n's great glory shone around
  The little earthborn child.

On earth they missed the little one—
  They sighed and wept and cried,
And wondered if another such
  As theirs had ever died.

Oh, had they seen through these high gates
  The welcome to him given,
They never would have wished their child
  Back from his home in Heaven!

        —Author unknown

WE'LL MEET AGAIN

Where do our loved ones go
   After life's last "good-bye"?
Is there a Home beyond
   Where they shall never die?

Questions like these arise,
   Challenging thoughtful men.
It is my firm belief,
   I shall see them again.

To that Fair Land unknown,
   Far from this earthly shore,
God calls His loved ones Home
   To life forevermore.

They shall be happy there,
   Dwelling above with Him,
And when He calls me, I believe,
   I shall know them again.

—Author unknown

NO ONE EXPECTED ME!

I dreamed death came the other night
  And Heaven's gate swung wide.
With kindly grace an angel came
  And welcomed me inside.

Well, there to my astonishment
  Stood folks I knew on earth.
Some I had judged and called unfit;
  Some were of little worth.

Indignant words rose to my lips
  But never were set free;
For every face showed stunned surprise—
  No one expected *me!*

—Selected

WHEN LOVED ONES GO BEFORE US

When loved ones go before us,
  We may feel that we're alone;
But there is still another life
  We haven't yet been shown.

For there's a bright and happy world
  That we are meant to see,
When we too learn that death is birth—
  Into eternity.

—Author unknown

IN REMEMBRANCE

We do not lose the ones we love;
    They only go before,
Where there is everlasting life,
    And sorrow is no more.

There the soul will always live,
    And peace is everywhere.
We do not lose the ones we love;
    God takes them in His care.

—Anonymous

Faith, Trust

A STREAM OF TROUBLE

There's a stream of trouble across my path—
　　It's black and deep and wide;
Bitter the hour the future hath
　　When I cross its swelling tide.

But I sing and smile and say,
　　I will hope and trust always;
I'll bear the sorrow that comes tomorrow,
　　But I'll borrow none today.

—Selected

GOD'S LOVE—A VEIL

The love of God has hung a veil around tomorrow
That we may not its beauty see nor trouble borrow.
But, oh, 'tis sweeter far to trust His unseen hand
And know that all the path of life His wisdom planned.
I know not if tomorrow's way be steep or rough;
But when His hand is guiding me, that is enough.
And so, although the veil has hid tomorrow's way,
I walk with perfect faith and trust through each today.

—Anonymous

ONLY WAIT

When I cannot understand my Father's leading,
    And it seems to be but hard and cruel fate;
Still I hear that gentle whisper ever pleading,
    "God is working; God is faithful—
        ONLY WAIT."

When the promise seems to linger, long delaying,
    And I tremble, lest perhaps it come too late;
Still I hear that sweet-voiced angel ever saying,
    "Though it tarry, it is coming—
        ONLY WAIT."

—Anonymous

Go to the depths of God's promise
    And claim whatsoever ye will;
The blessings of God will not fail thee;
    His Word He will surely fulfill.

HE NEVER FAILETH

*"Jesus Christ the same yesterday, and to day,
and for ever."*—Heb. 13:8.

O thou of little faith,
   God has not failed thee yet!
When all looks dark and gloomy,
   Thou dost so soon forget—

Forget that He has led thee
   And gently cleared thy way;
On clouds has poured His sunshine
   And turned thy night to day.

And if He's helped thee hitherto,
   He will not fail thee now;
How it must wound His loving heart
   To see thy anxious brow!

Oh, doubt not any longer;
   To Him commit thy way,
Whom in the past thou trusted
   And is "the same...to day."

—Selected

BESIDE THE SILENT SEA

I know not what the future hath
 Of marvel or surprise,
Assured alone that life and death
 His mercy underlies.

And so beside the silent sea
 I wait the muffled oar;
No harm from Him can come to me
 On ocean or on shore.

I know not where His islands lift
 Their fronded palms in air;
I only know I cannot drift
 Beyond His love and care.

And Thou, O Lord, by whom are seen
 Thy creatures as they be,
Forgive me if too close I lean
 My human heart on Thee.

     —Author unknown

I KNOW WHO HOLDS THE FUTURE

I know who holds the future,
 And I know He holds my hand;
With God things don't just happen—
 Ev'rything by Him is planned;
So as I face tomorrow
 With its problems large and small,
I'll trust the God of miracles—
 Give to Him my all.

     —Alfred B. Smith

NOT SO IN HASTE, MY HEART

Not so in haste, my heart!
   Have faith in God and wait;
Although He lingers long,
   He never comes too late.

He never cometh late;
   He knoweth what is best;
Vex not thyself in vain;
   Until He cometh, rest.

Until He cometh, rest,
   Nor grudge the hours that roll;
The feet that wait for God
   Are soonest at the goal;

Are soonest at the goal
   That is not gained by speed;
Then hold thee still, my heart,
   For I shall wait His lead.

—Bradford Torrey

EVER, ONLY JESUS

I've tried in vain a thousand ways
My fears to quell, my hopes to raise;
But what I need, the Bible says,
   Is ever, only Jesus.

My soul is night, my heart is steel,
I cannot see, I cannot feel;
For light, for life, I must appeal
   In simple faith to Jesus.

He died, He lives, He reigns, He pleads;
There's love in all His words and deeds;
There's all a guilty sinner needs
   Forevermore in Jesus.

Though some should sneer and some should blame,
I'll go with all my guilt and shame;
I'll go to Him because His name,
   Above all names, is Jesus.

            —Selected

FAITH

Faith is a thread,
Slender and frail,
  Easy to tear.
Yet it can lift
The weight of a soul
  Up from despair.

—Selected

I DO NOT ASK THAT HE MUST PROVE

I do not ask that He must prove
  His love is true to me,
And that before I can believe
  He first must let me see.
It is enough for me to know
'Tis true because He says 'tis so.
On His unchanging Word I'll stand—
And trust till I can understand.

—Selected

THIS I KNOW

I do not know what next may come
  Across my pilgrim way;
I do not know tomorrow's road,
  Nor see beyond today.
But this I know—my Saviour knows
  The path I cannot see;
And I can trust His wounded hand
  To guide and care for me.

I do not know what may befall
  Of sunshine or of rain;
I do not know what may be mine
  Of pleasure and of pain;
But this I know—my Saviour knows,
  And whatsoe'er it be,
Still I can trust His love to give
  What will be best for me.

I do not know what may await,
  Or what the morrow brings;
But with the glad salute of faith,
  I hail its opening wings;
For this I know—that in my Lord
  Shall all my needs be met;
And I can trust the heart of Him
  Who has not failed me yet.

—E. Margaret Clarkson

PERFECT PEACE

I don't look back; God knows the fruitless efforts,
　The wasted hours, the sinning, the regrets;
I leave them all with Him who blots the record
　And mercifully forgives and then forgets.

I don't look forward; God sees all the future,
　The road that, short or long, will lead me Home;
And He will face with me its every trial
　And bear for me the burdens that may come.

I don't look round me; then would fears assail me,
　So wild the tumult of earth's restless seas,
So dark the world, so filled with woe and evil,
　So vain the hope of comfort or of ease.

I don't look in, for then am I most wretched;
　My self hath naught on which to stay my trust.
Nothing I see save failures and shortcomings,
　And weak endeavors crumbling into dust.

But I look up...into the face of Jesus,
　For there my heart can rest, my fears are stilled;
And there is joy and love, and light for darkness,
　And perfect peace and every hope fulfilled.

　　　　　　　　　　　—Annie Johnson Flint

I'VE DREAMED MANY DREAMS

I've dreamed many dreams that never came true;
   I've seen them vanish at dawn;
But I've realized enough of my dreams, thank God,
   To make me want to dream on.

I've prayed many prayers when no answer came,
   Though I waited patient and long;
But answers have come to enough of my prayers
   To make me keep praying on.

I've trusted many a friend who failed
   And left me to weep alone;
But I've found enough of my friends true-blue
   To make me keep trusting on.

I've sown many seeds that fell by the way
   For the birds to feed upon;
But I've held enough golden sheaves in my hand
   To make me keep sowing on.

I've drained the cup of disappointment and pain
   And gone many days without song;
But I've sipped enough nectar from the roses of life
   To make me want to live on.

                —Author unknown

Guidance

AT THE PLACE OF THE SEA

Have you come to the Red Sea place in your life,
  Where, in spite of all you can do,
There is no way out, there is no way back,
  There is no other way but—through?
Then wait on the Lord with a trust serene
  Till the night of your fear is gone;
He will send the wind, He will heap the floods,
  When He says to your soul—"Go on."

And His hand will lead you through—clear through—
  Ere the watery walls roll down,
No foe can reach you, nor wave can touch,
  No mightiest sea can drown;
The tossing billows may rear their crests,
  Their foam at your feet may break,
But over their bed you shall walk dry-shod
  In the path that your Lord will make.

In the morning watch, 'neath the lifted cloud,
  You shall see but the Lord alone,
When He leads you on from the place of the sea
  To land that you have not known;
And your fears shall pass as your foes have passed;
  You shall be no more afraid;
You shall sing His praise in a better place,
  A place that His hand has made.

—Annie Johnson Flint

GOD'S CALL

Among the things that this day brings
    Will come to you a call,
The which unless you're listening
    You may not hear at all.
Lest it be very soft and low,
Whate'er you do, where'er you go,
      Be listening.

When God shall come and say to you,
"This is the thing that you must do,"
      Be listening.

—Selected

MY GUIDE

I do not know what lies ahead,
    The way I cannot see;
Yet One stands near to be my Guide—
    He'll show the way to me.

—Author unknown

STEP BY STEP

He does not lead me year by year,
    Nor even day by day,
But step by step my path unfolds;
    My Lord directs my way.

Tomorrow's plans I do not know—
    I only know this minute.
But He will say, "This is the way;
    By faith now walk ye in it."

And I am glad that it is so;
    Today's enough to bear.
And when tomorrow comes, His grace
    Shall far exceed its care.

What need to worry then or fret?
    The God who gave His Son
Holds all my moments in His hand
    And gives them one by one.

—Barbara C. Ryberg

Home

THE HEART OF A CHILD

Whatever you write on the heart of a child,
    No water can wash away.
The sand may be shifted when billows are wild,
    And the efforts of time may decay.

Some stories may perish,
    Some songs be forgot;
But this graven record—
    Time changes not.

Whatever you write on the heart of a child,
    A story of gladness or care,
That Heaven has blessed, or earth has defiled,
    Will linger unchangeably there.
Who writes it has sealed it forever and aye,
He must answer to God on the judgment day.

—Author unknown

*"Train up a child in the way he should go: and when he is
old, he will not depart from it."*—Prov. 22:6.

"I'LL BE LIKE YOU!"

His little arms crept round my neck,
   And then I heard him say
Four simple words I can't forget,
   Four words that made me pray.

They turned a mirror on my soul,
   On secrets no one knew;
They startled me; I hear them yet:
   Said he, "I'll be like you!"

              —Author unknown

MOTHERS

Of all the gifts God ever gave,
　　There's one above all others;
He never gave us quite so much
　　As when He gave us mothers.

Of all the prizes that we won,
　　There's one we'll love forever;
The gift we know as mother's love,
　　No power on earth can sever.

Of all the treasures that we have,
　　There's one we hold more dearly;
Next to our precious Saviour's love,
　　We love her most sincerely.

O God above, we thank Thee for
　　The mothers of all nations;
Protect them with Thy steady hand
　　And give them Your salvation.

　　　　　　　　—Selected

ONLY A DAD

Only a dad, with a tired face,
Coming home from the daily race,
Bringing little of gold or fame
To show how well he has played the game,
But great in his heart that his own rejoice
To see him coming, to hear his voice.

Only a dad, with a brood of four,
One of ten million men or more,
Plodding along in the daily strife,
Bearing the whips and the scorns of life
With never a whimper of pain or hate
For the sake of those who at home await.

Only a dad, neither rich nor proud,
Merely one of the searching crowd,
Toiling, striving from day to day,
Facing whatever may come his way,
Silent whenever the harsh condemn,
And bearing it all for the love of them.

Only a dad, but he gives his all
To smooth the way for his children small;
To do with courage stern and grim
The deeds that his father did for him.
This is the line that for him I pen—
Only a dad, but the best of men.

—Author unknown

Praise and Thanksgiving

MY DEBT

When I stand before the throne,
Dressed in beauty not my own;
When I see Thee as Thou art,
Love Thee with unsinning heart;
Then, Lord, shall I fully know—
Not 'til then—how much I owe.

Chosen not for good in me,
Wakened up from wrath to flee;
Hidden in the Saviour's side,
By the Spirit sanctified.
Teach me, Lord, on earth to show
By my love how much I owe.

—R. M. McCheyne

Prayer

A MATTER OF PRAYER

When you are weary in body and soul,
    Cumbered with many a care,
When work is claiming its strength-taking toll,
    Make it a matter of prayer.

When you're discouraged, distraught or dismayed,
    Sinking almost in despair,
Remember, there's One who will come to your aid,
    If you'll make it a matter of prayer.

And when you are lost in the world's tangled maze,
    When life seems a hopeless affair,
Direction will come for all of your ways
    If you'll make it a matter of prayer.

—Author unknown

A LITTLE TALK

Just a little talk with Jesus,
    How it smooths the rugged road;
How it cheers and helps me onward
    When I faint beneath the load!

When my heart is crushed with sorrow
    And my eyes with tears are dim,
There's naught can yield me comfort
    Like a little talk with Him.

—Anonymous

Salvation

PRISONERS OUT OF THE PIT

How sad our state by nature is!
    Our sin—how deep it stains!
And Satan holds our captive minds
    Fast in his slavish chains.

But there's a voice of sovereign grace,
    Sounds from the sacred Word:
"Ho! ye despairing sinners, come
    And trust a pardoning Lord."

My soul obeys the almighty call,
    And runs to this relief;
I would believe Thy promise, Lord:
    Oh, help my unbelief!

A guilty, weak and helpless worm,
    On Thy strong arms I fall.
Be Thou my Strength and Righteousness,
    My Saviour and my All.

—Isaac Watts

THE TOUCH OF THE MASTER'S HAND

'Twas battered and scarred, and the auctioneer
Thought it scarcely worth his while
To waste much time on the old violin,
But held it up with a smile:
"What am I bidden, good folks," he cried;
"Who'll start the bidding for me?"
"A dollar, a dollar"; then, "Two!" "Only two?
Two dollars, and who'll make it three?
Three dollars, once; three dollars, twice;
Going for three—" But no,
From the room, far back, a gray-haired man
Came forward and picked up the bow;
Then, wiping the dust from the old violin,
And tightening the loosened strings,
He played a melody pure and sweet
As a caroling angel sings.

The music ceased, and the auctioneer,
With a voice that was quiet and low,
Said, "Now what am I bid for the old violin?"
And he held it up with the bow.
"A thousand dollars, and who'll make it two?
Two thousand? And who'll make it three?
Three thousand, once; three thousand, twice,
And going, and gone!" cried he.
The people cheered, but some of them cried,
"We do not quite understand;
What changed its worth?" Swift came the reply:
"The touch of the master's hand."

And many a man with life out of tune,
And battered and scarred with sin,
Is auctioned cheap to a thoughtless crowd,
Much like the old violin.

A "mess of pottage," a glass of wine;
A game—and he travels on.
He's "going" once, and "going" twice,
He's "going," and almost "gone"!
But the Master comes, and the foolish crowd
Never can quite understand
The worth of a soul and the change that's wrought
By the touch of the Master's hand.

—Myra Brooks Welch

"THEN COMETH HE"

John 4:5

Andrew and Peter were disciples of John
Who pointed to Another, saying, "I'm not the one."
They looked as they walked by blue Galilee,
Beheld a Lamb...
           "Then cometh he."

A blind man sits in darkness, alone—
His hope and courage almost gone.
And all he desires is just to see.
The morning breaks...
           "Then cometh he."

A woman comes to Jacob's well.
Her sin-scarred face a sad story could tell.
She came—a thirsty sinner was she,
Hopeless, helpless...
           "Then cometh he."

A maniac no man could tame
Would curse and mock the Lord's dear name,
But then he's found at the Master's knee.
"Why?" we ask...
           "Then cometh he."

Two sisters weep as their hearts do break.
Their brother, Lazarus, will not awake;
But their sorrow is soon turned to glee
Because at the tomb...
           "Then cometh he."

A man came by night, confused within.
He could not rid himself of sin;

He wished to know, he wished to see
How he "born again" could be...
            "Then cometh he."

And many a sinner desires the same.
He tries to find peace in wealth and fame,
But joy and hope just seem to flee
Until at last...
            "Then cometh he."

He satisfies our thirsty soul.
With just a word He makes us whole;
And we thank God at last we're free,
And it's all because...
            "Then cometh he."

—Clyde H. Box

MY FAITH HAS FOUND A RESTING PLACE

My faith has found a resting place,
    Not in device nor creed;
I trust the ever living One,
    His wounds for me shall plead.

Enough for me that Jesus saves,
    This ends my fear and doubt;
A sinful soul I come to Him,
    He'll never cast me out.

My heart is leaning on the Word,
    The written Word of God,
Salvation by my Saviour's name,
    Salvation through His blood.

My great Physician heals the sick,
    The lost He came to save;
For me His precious blood He shed,
    For me His life He gave.

I need no other argument,
    I need no other plea;
It is enough that Jesus died,
    And that He died for me.

—Lidie H. Edmunds

THAT DAY AT CALVARY

I stood one day at Calvary,
　Where Jesus bled and died.
I never knew He loved me so,
　For me was crucified.
And as I stood there in my sin,
　His love reached down to me.
And, oh, the shame that filled my soul
　That day at Calvary.

I knelt one day at Calvary;
　My eyes were filled with tears
To think such love I have refused
　Throughout these wasted years.
And as I knelt I heard Him say,
　"I did it all for thee";
And, oh, the shame that filled my soul
　That day at Calvary.

I prayed one day at Calvary,
　"I'm Thine forevermore;
Forgive me, Lord, for all my sins;
　My lost estate restore."
And as I prayed, to me He gave
　Salvation full and free;
And, oh, the peace that filled my soul
　That day at Calvary.

—Anonymous

SOMEBODY WHISPERED THAT JESUS LOVES ME

One day in sin I was told of a love
Coming from One who is reigning above.
Gladly I listened—'twas music to me
To know, though a sinner, that I could be free.

Now that I tasted this love so sublime,
Jesus abideth within all the time;
Joybells are ringing, 'tis heaven below;
Wherever He leadeth I gladly will go.

Now I am telling the story so sweet.
Service for Jesus makes earth joys complete;
Walking and talking with Him all the way,
For Jesus grows sweeter and sweeter each day.

Somebody whispered that Jesus loves me—
Jesus who died upon Calvary's tree;
Said He would save me, from sin set me free;
Somebody whispered that Jesus loves me.

—Scott Lawrence

"WHOSOEVER"

I am in that "whosoever";
I believe He died for me.
Praise the Lord, I'm saved forever!
Jesus lives! And I am free!

—Selected

THE MYSTERY OF GRACE

In evil long I took delight,
    Unawed by shame or fear,
Till a new object struck my sight
    And stopped my wild career.

I saw One hanging on a tree
    In agony and blood;
He fixed His languid eyes on me,
    As near His cross I stood.

Sure never, till my latest breath,
    Can I forget that look;
It seemed to charge me with His death,
    Tho' not a word He spoke.

My conscience felt and owned the guilt
    And plunged me in despair;
I saw my sins His blood had spilt
    And helped to nail Him there.

A second look He gave, which said,
    "I freely all forgive.
This blood is for thy ransom paid;
    I die that thou may'st live."

Thus, while His death my sin displays
    In all its blackest hue,
Such is the mystery of grace;
    It seals my pardon too.

—John Newton

A YEARNING FOR HIM

You ask me how I gave my heart to Christ—
    I do not know;
There came a yearning in my soul for Him
    So long ago.

I found earth's flowers would fade and die.
I wept for something that could not satisfy.
And then...and then...somehow I seemed to dare
To lift my broken heart to Him in prayer.

I do not know...I cannot tell you how:
I only know that He's my Saviour now.

                  —Author unknown

MY GIFT

What can I give Him
    Poor as I am?
If I were a shepherd,
    I would give Him a lamb.
If I were a wise man,
    I would do my part.
But what can I give Him?
    Give my heart.

              —Christina Rossetti

THE VOICE OF GOD REGARD

Sinner, the voice of God regard;
    'Tis mercy speaks today;
He calls you by His sacred Word
    From sin's destructive way.

Why will you in the crooked ways
    Of sin and folly go?
In pain you travel all your days
    To reach eternal woe.

But he who turns to God shall live
    Through His abounding grace;
He in mercy will the guilt forgive
    Of those who seek His face.

—Author unknown

Second Coming

HE IS COMING

He is coming! He is coming!
    You can almost hear the sound
Of His footsteps at the threshold,
    And our hearts with gladness bound.

All around us men are seeking,
    Turning blind eyes to the light,
Longing, fearing, not yet daring
    To escape from sin's dark night.

Yet the message is so simple:
    "I will surely come again."
'Tis the glad news of the Gospel
    Ringing sweetly through earth's pain.

When He comes, may I be ready,
    Watching, praying, working still.
Though He tarry, may I daily
    Learn more perfectly His will.

—Author unknown

THE ONLY THING THAT KEEPS ME UP

The only thing that keeps me up
    While tears are flowing free
Is that my Lord is coming soon
    To bless and comfort me!

—Author unknown

Service and Soul Winning

THE BRIDGE BUILDER

An old man, traveling a lone highway,
Came at evening, cold and gray,
To a chasm vast and deep and wide,
Through which was flowing a sullen tide.
The old man crossed in the twilight dim,
For the sullen stream held no fears for him,
But he turned when he reached the other side,
And builded a bridge to span the tide.

"Old man," cried a fellow pilgrim near,
"You are wasting your strength with building here;
Your journey will end with the closing day;
And you never again will pass this way.
You have crossed the chasm deep and wide.
Why build you a bridge at eventide?"

And the builder lifted his old gray head:
"Good friend, on the path I have come," he said,
"There followeth after me today
A youth whose feet must pass this way.
This stream, which has been as naught to me,
To that fair-haired boy may a pitfall be;
He too must cross in the twilight dim—
Good friend, I am building this bridge for him."

—W. A. Dromgoole

WHAT IS IN THY HAND?

What hast thou in thy hand,
   Woman? "One handful" more.
Go feed the prophet, and 'twill last
   Till famine days are o'er.

What hast thou in thy hand,
   Widow? "A pot of oil."
Go pour it out and find a store
   Of rich and priceless spoil.

What hast thou in thy hand,
   Mary? Some "perfume rare."
Pour it upon His head; 'twill flow
   In fragrance everywhere.

And, Dorcas, what hast thou?
   "A needle and some thread."
Give them to God; they'll bless the poor,
   And bring thee from the dead.

What hast thou in thy hand,
   Widow? "Two mites"—no more.
Give them to God, and they shall grow
   To be a mighty store.

What hast thou in thy hand,
   Mother? "A baby's hand."
Train him for God, so shall thy light
   Bear fruit in every land.

What hast thou in thy hand,
   Teacher? "A child's young mind."
Teach him to live for God and man;
   So shalt thou bless mankind.

What hast thou in thy hand,
   Writer? "A common pen."
Use it to write His messages
   Upon the hearts of men.

          —Selected

SMILE

The thing that goes the farthest
   Towards making life worthwhile,
Which costs the least and counts the most
   Is just a pleasant smile.
The smile that bubbles from a heart
   That loves its fellowmen
Will drive away the clouds of gloom
   And coax the sun again.
It's full of worth and goodness too,
   With manly kindness blent;
It's worth a million dollars,
   And it doesn't cost a cent.

There is no room for sadness
   When we see a cheery smile;
It always has the same good looks—
   It's never out of style.
It nerves us on to try again
   When failure makes us blue;
The dimples of encouragement
   Are good for me and you.
It pays a higher interest,
   For it is merely lent—
It's worth a million dollars
   And doesn't cost a cent.

A smile comes very easy—
   You can wrinkle up with cheer
A hundred times before you can
   Squeeze out a soggy tear.
It ripples out, moreover,
   To the heartstrings that will tug,
And always leaves an echo
   That is very like a hug;

So, smile away. Folks understand
   What by a smile is meant;
It's worth a million dollars
   And doesn't cost a cent.

           —Selected

THE PREACHER'S WIFE

There is one person in our church
  Who knows our preacher's life,
Who wept and smiled and prayed with him;
  And that's the preacher's wife.

The crowd has seen him in his strength,
  When wielding God's sharp sword,
As underneath God's banner folds
  He faced the Devil's horde.

But deep within her heart she knows
  That scarce an hour before,
She helped him pray the glory down
  Behind the closet door.

She's heard him groaning in his soul
  When bitter raged the strife,
As hand in hand she knelt with him—
  For she's the preacher's wife!

You tell your tales of prophets brave
  Who marched across the world
And changed the course of history
  By burning words they hurled—

And I will tell you back of each
  Some woman lived her life;
Who wept with him and smiled with him—
  She was the preacher's wife!

  —Author unknown

TELL HIM NOW

If with pleasure you are viewing
Any work a man is doing;
   If you like him or you love him, tell him now.
Don't withhold your approbation
Till the parson makes oration
   And he lies with snowy lilies o'er his brow.

For no matter how you shout it,
He won't really care about it;
   He won't know how many teardrops you have shed.
If you think some praise is due him,
Now's the time to slip it to him,
   For he cannot read the tombstone when he's dead.

More than fame and more than money
Is the comment kind and sunny,
   And the hearty, warm approval of a friend;
For it gives to life a savor,
Makes you richer, stronger, braver,
   And it gives you heart and courage to the end.

If he earns your praise, bestow it,
If you like him, let him know it,
   Let the words of true encouragement be said;
Do not wait till life is over,
And he's underneath the clover,
   For he cannot read the tombstone when he's dead.

—F. W. Brazier

DO IT!

If you have anything to say,
True and needed, yea or nay—
    Say it!

If you have anything to give
That another's joy may live—
    Give it!

If you have any debt to pay,
Rest you neither night or day—
    Pay it!

If you have anything to do,
Let me whisper, friend, to you—
    Do it!

"Whatsoever he saith unto you, do it."—John 2:5.

BEGIN TODAY

Dream not too much of what you'll do tomorrow,
  How well you'll work another year;
Tomorrow's chance you do not need to borrow—
      Today is here.

Boast not too much of mountains you will master,
  The while you linger in the vale below.
To dream is well, but plodding brings us faster
      To where we go.

Talk not too much about some new endeavor
  You mean to make a little later on.
Who idles now will idle on forever
      Till life is gone.

Swear not someday to break some habit's fetters,
  When this old year is dead and passed away;
If you have need of living wiser, better,
      Begin today!

                    —Anonymous

OTHERS

Lord, help me live from day to day
In such a self-forgetful way
That even when I kneel to pray,
   My prayer shall be for others.

Help me in all the work I do
To ever be sincere and true
And know that all I do for You
   Must needs be done for others.

Let self be crucified and slain
And buried deep, and all in vain
May efforts be to rise again,
   Unless to live for others.

And when my work on earth is done
And my new work in Heaven begun,
May I forget the crown I won
   While thinking still of others.

Others, Lord, yes others,
   Let this my motto be;
Help me to live for others
   That I may live like Thee.

         —Charles D. Meigs

A LOVE FOR SOULS

Oh, give me, Lord, Thy love for souls—
    For lost and wandering sheep—
That I may see the multitudes
    And weep as Thou didst weep.

Help me to see the tragic plight
    Of souls far off in sin.
Help me to love, to pray, to go
    And bring the wanderer in.

From off the altar of Thy heart
    Take Thou some flaming coals;
Then touch my life and give me, Lord,
    A heart that's hot for souls.

Oh, fire of love; oh, flame divine,
    Make Thy abode in me;
Burn in my heart, burn evermore
    'Til I burn out for Thee.

—Eugene M. Harrison

THE CLOCK OF LIFE

The clock of life is wound but once,
  And no man has the power
To tell just when the hands will stop,
  At late or early hour.
Now is the only time you own;
  Live, love, toil with a will;
Place no faith in tomorrow, for—
  The clock may then be still.

—Author unknown

To dwell above with the saints we love—
  That will be grace and glory.
To dwell below with the saints we know—
  Ah...that's a different story!

Sin

THE BEAUTIFUL SNOW

In the early part of the Civil War, one dark Saturday morning in the dead of winter there died at the Commercial Hospital, Cincinnati, a young woman over whose head only two and twenty summers had passed. She had once been possessed of an enviable share of beauty; had been, as she herself said, "flattered and sought for the charm of her face." But alas! upon her fair brow had long been written that terrible word—*fallen!*

Once the pride of respectable parentage, her first wrong step was the sad beginning of the "same old story over again," which has been, alas, the painful history of thousands. Highly educated and accomplished in manner, she might have shone in a prominent circle. But the evil hour that proved to be the beginning of her fall was like the door leading out of the innocency of childhood and modesty of youth into vice and ruin. And having spent a young life in disgrace and shame, the poor friendless one died the melancholy death of a brokenhearted outcast.

Among her personal effects was found, in manuscript, "The Beautiful Snow," which was immediately carried to a gentleman of culture and literary tastes, who was at that time editor of the *National Union*. In the columns of that paper, on the morning following the girl's death, the poem appeared in print for the first time. When the paper containing the poem came out on Sunday morning, the body of the victim of sin had not yet received burial. The attention of one of the first American poets was soon directed to the newly published lines, who was so taken with their stirring pathos that he immediately sought for and followed the corpse to its final resting-place.

Oh, the snow! the beautiful snow,
Filling the sky and earth below!
Over the housetops, over the street,
Over the heads of the people you meet,
   Dancing—
         Flirting—
               Skimming along.
Beautiful snow! it can do no wrong;
Flying to kiss a fair lady's cheek;
Clinging to lips in frolicsome freak.
Beautiful snow from the heavens above,
Pure as an angel, gentle as love.
Oh, the snow! the beautiful snow!
How the flakes gather and laugh as they go
Whirling about in its maddening fun;
It plays in its glee with every one.
   Chasing—
         Laughing—
               Hurrying by,
It lights on the face, and it sparkles the eye;
And playful dogs with a bark and a bound
Snap at the crystals that eddy around.
The town is alive, and its heart is aglow,
To welcome the coming of beautiful snow!
How the wild crowd goes swaying along,
Hailing each other with humor and song!
How the gay sleighs like meteors flash by,
Bright for a moment, then lost to the eye.
   Ringing—
         Swinging—
               Dashing they go,
Over the crest of the beautiful snow,
Snow so pure when it falls from the sky,
As to make one regret to see it lie
To be trampled and tracked by thousands of feet,
Till it blends with the horrible filth in the street.

Once I was pure as the snow, but I fell:
Fell, like the snowflakes from Heaven—to Hell;
Fell, to be trampled as filth of the street;
Fell, to be scoffed, to be spit on and beat.
   Pleading—
       Cursing—
          Dreading to die,
Selling my soul to whoever would buy.
Dealing in shame for a morsel of bread,
Hating the living and fearing the dead.
Merciful God! have I fallen so low?
And yet I was once like the beautiful snow!

Once I was fair as the beautiful snow,
With an eye like its crystals, a heart like its glow;
Once I was loved for my innocent grace—
Flattered and sought for the charm of my face,
   Father—
       Mother—
          Sisters—all:
God and myself I have lost by my fall!
The veriest wretch that goes shivering by
Will keep a wide sweep lest I wander too nigh;
For of all that is on or about me, I know,
There is nothing that's pure—but the beautiful snow.
How strange it should be that this beautiful snow
Should fall on a sinner with nowhere to go!
How strange it would be, when the night comes
   again,
If the snow and the ice struck my desperate brain;
   Fainting—
       Freezing—
          Dying alone—
Too wicked for prayer, too weak for my moan
To be heard in the crash of the crazy town

Gone mad in the joy at the snow's coming down;—
To lie and to die in my terrible woe,
With a bed and a shroud of the beautiful snow!

—Author unknown

(Last verse written by a servant of the Lord)

Helpless and foul as the trampled snow,
Sinner, despair not! Christ stoopeth low
To rescue the soul that is lost in sin,
And raise it to life and enjoyment again.
   Groaning—
         Bleeding—
               Dying for thee,
The Crucified hung on th' accursed tree!
His accents of mercy fall soft on thine ear:
"There is mercy for thee";—He will hear thy weak
   prayer.
"O God, in the stream that for sinners did flow,
Wash me, and I shall be whiter than snow."

INDEX OF TITLES AND FIRST LINES

For a complete list of books available from the Sword of the Lord, write to Sword of the Lord Publishers, P. O. Box 1099, Murfreesboro, Tennessee 37133.

(800) 251-4100
(615) 893-6700
FAX (615) 848-6943
www.swordofthelord.com